COSMIC scallies

by Jackie Hagan

Cosmic Scallies was first produced by the Royal Exchange Theatre, Manchester, and Graeae Theatre Company and first performed as part of Northern Stage at Summerhall at the 2017 Edinburgh Festival Fringe on 5 August 2017.

INTRODUCTIONS

Society's view of the working classes has crumbled in my lifetime and we now live in a world where chav-shaming and poverty appropriation is commonplace. It's said that it takes a village to raise a baby – and our society as a village is failing, standing on the outskirts of love, judging when one person's trying doesn't look like your own.

Disability and class is linked, people get stressed and get sick. The community of Skelmersdale helps those who need it; I'm not saying we're saints – we say bad words, we're tired, some of us are scallies, some of us have gone a bit cosmic inside our own heads in order to get by. But there's more compassion than people from outside of Skem seem to think.

There isn't much of a class system in Skem, there's just people with slightly nicer shoes, so when I was young I didn't realise people lived differently from us. People on telly were just a daydream; surely no one actually went to Disneyland? But now that kids are plugged into YouTube and drip-fed plastic aspiration 24/7, I feel for the ones who are gonna have to try harder or to accept disappointment. *Cosmic Scallies* is a love letter to Skem and the necessary ways we cope with not getting what we want.

Jackie Hagan, Writer

It's very rare to read a play that makes you laugh out loud again, again and again. *Cosmic Scallies* does just that. On the surface not a lot happens but so much is said that articulates the experience of the People's Republic of Skelmersdale. Dent and Shaun are two complex, lovable, frustrating characters whose voices are still marginalised, misunderstood and misrepresented. And I'm not even talking about the theatre here. It's a tribute to Jackie that she's funnily crafted a piece of work that has the potential to make you laugh and wind you within a sentence or two of dialogue.

Dent and Shaun are trying to live day by day. They are lonely in familiar surroundings. They are trying to negotiate a world which continues to fail them, and in turn, they fail their world. They have to learn to trust each other, work with each other, tell each other as it is because they have more things that unite than divide. It's a message that can be transported from Skem to planet Earth. Be what you want to be but don't be snooty. It's not very Cosmic and the Scallies will have ya!

Amit Sharma, Director

CAST

DENT   **Rachel Denning**
SHAUN   **Reuben Johnson**

CREATIVE TEAM

Director	**Amit Sharma**
Dramaturg	**Jeff Young**
Designer	**Bethany Wells**
Lighting Designer	**Joshua Pharo**
Sound Designer	**Lewis Gibson**
Movement Director	**Chi-San Howard**
Voice Coach	**Elspeth Morrison**
Assistant Director	**James Varney**

PRODUCTION TEAM

Production Manager	**Richard Delight**
Casting	**Jerry Knight Smith** CDG
Company Stage Manager	**Philip Hussey**
Wardrobe Supervisor	**Felicia Jagne**
Workshop Supervisor	**Carl Heston**
LX Supervisor	**Mark Distin-Webster**
Sound Supervisor	**Sorcha Williams**
Set, costumes and props by	**Royal Exchange Theatre**
Audio Description Consultant/ Access Worker	**Wayne 'Pickles' Norman**
Audio Describer	**Mandy Colleran**
Access Workers	**Suzanna Hamilton**
	Narinder Samra
Cover Photography	**Gu Photography**
Title Artwork	**Dragonfly Design**

BIOGRAPHIES

SHAUN | **REUBEN JOHNSON**
Theatre includes: *The Darkest Corners* (Transform Festival); *A Streetcar Named Desire, Come Closer* (Royal Exchange Theatre); *On Corporation Street* (HOME); *The Iliad* (Royal Lyceum Theatre); *Gary: A Love Story* (24:7 Theatre Festival); *The C Project, Wrecked* (Lowry); *Territory* (Pleasance Islington); *The Meeting* (Pleasance Edinburgh). Television and film includes: *The City and The City* (Mammoth Screen/BBC); *Loaded* (Hillbilly Films); *The Aliens* (Clerkenwell Films); *Doctor Who, Doctors, Casualty, Prisoners' Wives* (BBC); *Weekender* (Momentum Pictures); *Territory* (Fiddy West Productions); *Postcards from London* (Diablo Films).

DENT | **RACHEL DENNING**
Theatre includes: *Dr Frankenstein* (Northern Stage); *The Government Inspector* (Birmingham Rep); *Redefining Juliet* (Barbican); *The Vote* (Donmar Warehouse); *See How They Run* (Reduced Height Theatre Company); *Curious Curios* (Kazzum); *Volpone* (Fire Under The Horizon); *Speakeasy Monologue Evening* (Insignificant Theatre); *Story Whores* (paper/scissors/stone); *Dick Whittington* (Chaplins). Television includes: *Doctor Who, Call the Midwife, Life's Too Short* (BBC); *The Vote* (Donmar/More4).

WRITER | **JACKIE HAGAN**

Jackie Hagan is from a forgotten new town (Skelmersdale, in which *Cosmic Scallies* is set) that the *Guardian* called 'a waking nightmare'; she loved it. She is a theatre-maker, playwright, poet and performer; shedding light on life as a working-class woman in a small town. She is also a queer amputee who downs champagne from her glittery false leg and dresses her stump up as celebrities in her cabaret act. This year she was the recipient of a Jerwood Compton Poetry Fellowship. Last year she represented the UK in FLUPP international poetry slam in Rio de Janeiro and was the focus of a Channel 4 documentary. The previous year she won the Best Spoken Word Show Saboteur Award for her first solo show *Some People Have Too Many Legs*, and a Creative Futures Award for literature. For the past ten years she has run a not-for-profit organisation providing workshops, support and opportunities for isolated adults. Jackie is a graduate from Graeae's flagship writer development programme *Write to Play*.

DIRECTOR | **AMIT SHARMA**

Director Amit Sharma has been Associate Director at Graeae since 2011 and is currently at the Royal Exchange Theatre as Associate Artistic Director. Amit's last production, *The Solid Life of Sugar Water*, received unanimous four- and five-star reviews and won the Euan's Guide Most Accessible Show of the Fringe Award in 2015 and transferred to the National Theatre's Temporary Space in spring 2016. Other directing credits for Graeae include *Prometheus Awakes* and *The Iron Man* (UK tour). While at Graeae, Amit led the *Write to Play* programme.

DESIGNER | **BETHANY WELLS**

Bethany Wells is a designer for dance, theatre and installation, with a particular focus on site-specific and devised performance. Recent work includes: *Party Skills for the End of the World* (Nigel Barrett and Louise Mari, Manchester International Festival); *All We Ever Wanted Was Everything* (Middle Child); *Removal Men* (Yard Theatre); *Dark Corners* (Polar Bear); *Seen and Not Heard* (Complicite Creative Learning); *The Future* (Company Three); *The Factory* (Royal Exchange Young Company); *Partus* (Third Angel). An ongoing project is *Other Acts of Public WARMTH*, a wood-fired mobile sauna and performance space, commissioned by Compass Live Art + touring nationally.

LIGHTING & CAPTIONING DESIGNER | **JOSHUA PHARO**

Joshua Pharo works as a Lighting and Projection Designer across theatre, dance, opera, music, film & art installation. Recent credits include: *Bodies* (Royal Court); *How My Light is Spent* (Royal Exchange Theatre); *The Bear & The Proposal* (Young Vic); *Scarlett* (Hampstead Theatre/Theatr Clywd); *Years of Sunlight* (Theatre503); *The Twits* (Curve Theatre/tour); *Removal Men* (Yard Theatre); *Broken Biscuits* (Paines Plough); *The Future* (Company Three); *Contractions* (Sheffield Crucible); *Julie* (Northern Stage); *We're Stuck!* (China Plate); *Giving* (Hampstead); *Iphigenia Quartet, In The Night Time (Before the Sun Rises), Medea* (Gate Theatre); *The Rolling Stone* (Orange Tree Theatre); *The Crocodile* (MFI); *One Arm, Usagi Yojimbo* (Southwark Playhouse).

SOUND DESIGNER & COMPOSER | **LEWIS GIBSON**

Lewis Gibson studied music at Dartington College of Arts. He has been a long-term collaborator with Graeae, writing music and designing sound for a number of their productions including *The Solid Life of Sugar Water, Reasons to be Cheerful, The Iron Man, Belonging, The Limbless Knight* and *The Garden*. He is an associate artist with Uninvited Guests (*The Lost Palace, Make Better Please, It Is Like It Ought To Be; A Pastoral*) and a founding member of the international touring company SABAB (*Ur, In The Eruptive Mode, The Speaker's Progress, Richard III: An Arab Tragedy, The Al-Hamlet Summit*). As a writer, director and composer he has made a number of pieces of young people's theatre with the Royal Exchange, Tangere Arts, Fuel and The Unicorn including *Tin Soldier* (winner OFFIE best young people's show 2012), *A Thousand Slimy Things, The Pardoner's Tale, The Chair* and *The Day I Fell Into A Book*. Other theatre includes Complicite, National Theatre (*A Pacifist's Guide to the War on Cancer*), The Young Vic, Nigel and Louise, Battersea Arts Centre and Cardboard Citizens.

MOVEMENT | **CHI-SAN HOWARD**

Chi-San Howard trained at the Royal Central School of Speech and Drama. Previous movement work for theatre: *Children of the Night* (Oxford Playhouse/Oxford Arts Festival); *These Trees Are Made of Blood* (Arcola Theatre); *Deposit* (*Associate,* Hampstead Theatre Downstairs); *Occupational Hazards* (*Associate,* Hampstead Theatre); *Moth* (Hope Mill Theatre); *Every You Every Me* (Oxford Playhouse); *The Tempest* (Southwark Playhouse); *Adding Machine: A Musical* (Finborough Theatre); *Scarlet* (Southwark Playhouse). Film work includes *Birds of Paradise* (Pemberton Films). Assistant Movement Director credits are: *Great Expectations* (West Yorkshire Playhouse); *Sweeney Todd: The Demon Barber of Fleet Street* (Welsh National Opera/West Yorkshire Playhouse).

GRAE*ae*

THEATRE COMPANY

Graeae is a force for change in world-class theatre – breaking down barriers, challenging preconceptions and boldly placing D/deaf and disabled artists centre stage. Artistically led by Jenny Sealey MBE, Graeae's signature characteristic is the compelling creative integration of sign language, audio description and captioning, which engages brilliantly with both disabled and non-disabled audiences. Championing accessibility and providing a platform for new generations of artists, Graeae leads the way in pioneering, trail-blazing theatre.

Recent productions include: *Reasons to be Cheerful* (retouring in 2017 in association with the Belgrade Theatre Coventry), *The House of Bernarda Alba* (in co-production with the Royal Exchange), *The Solid Life of Sugar Water* (in co-production with Theatre Royal Plymouth), *Blood Wedding* (in co-production with Dundee Rep Ensemble and Derby Theatre), *The Threepenny Opera* (in co-production with West Yorkshire Playhouse, New Wolsey Theatre Ipswich, Nottingham Playhouse Company and Birmingham Repertory Theatre), *Belonging* (in co-production with Circo Crescer e Viver), *Reasons to be Cheerful* and Sarah Kane's *Blasted*. Spectacular outdoor productions in recent years have included *The Limbless Knight – A Tale of Rights Reignited* (in association with Strange Fruit commissioned by GDIF), *Prometheus Awakes* (with la Fura dels Baus/co-commissioned by GDIF and SIRF) and *The Iron Man*.

Throughout the year, Graeae runs continuing professional development programmes as well as workshops and training programmes locally, nationally and internationally from Birmingham to Brazil to Bangladesh. Workshops and residencies widen participation and are run by our pool of Deaf and disabled facilitators in a variety of formal and informal education settings, helping to build new audiences, engage young creative minds and empower disabled artists.

CEO/Artistic Director **Jenny Sealey MBE**

Find out more & sign up to mailing list at
graeae.org
twitter @graeae
facebook.com/graeae

Graeae Registered Charity no 284589.
Graeae Theatre Company & Royal Exchange Theatre both gratefully acknowledge support from Arts Council England.

Manchester's Royal Exchange Theatre Company transforms the way people see theatre, each other and the world around them.

Its historic building, once the world's biggest cotton exchange, was taken over by artists in 1976. Today it is an award-winning cultural charity that produces new theatre in-the-round, in communities, on the road and online.

Exchange remains at the heart of everything they make and do. Now, their currency is brand new drama and reinvigorated classics, the boldest artists and a company of highly skilled makers – all brought together to trade ideas and experiences with the people of Greater Manchester (and beyond).

The Exchange's unique auditorium is powerfully democratic, a space where audiences and performers meet as equals, entering and exiting through the same doors. It inspires everything they do; inviting everyone to understand the past, engage in today's big questions, collectively imagine a better future and lose themselves in the moment of a great night out.

The Autumn Winter 2017/18 season is one of the biggest and most exciting ever with four World Premieres, including two Bruntwood Prize Winners. It opens with *Our Town* by Thornton Wilder, directed by Sarah Frankcom, *Parliament Square* by James Fritz, *Jubilee* – a brand-new stage adaptation of Derek Jarman's film, by Chris Goode, *Guys and Dolls* in a co-production with Talawa Theatre, *The Almighty Sometimes* by Kendall Feaver, *Cosmic Scallies* by Jackie Hagan in a co-production with Graeae Theatre, and *Black Men Walking* by Testament in a co-production with Eclipse Theatre Company.

Artistic Director   **Sarah Frankcom**
Executive Director   **Mark Dobson**
Associate Artistic Directors   **Matthew Xia, Amit Sharma**
Senior Producer   **Ric Watts**

royalexchange.co.uk

twitter @rxtheatre
instagram.com/rxtheatre
facebook.com/rxtheatre

Royal Exchange Theatre Registered Charity no.255424.

COSMIC SCALLIES

Jackie Hagan

Characters

DENT
SHAUN

This text went to press before the end of rehearsals and so may differ slightly from the play as performed.

Scene One

The flat. Afternoon. DENT *is getting ready to leave.* SHAUN *has just turned up.*

SHAUN. Dent! You little weirdo! Look at you back in your natural habitat!

DENT. My natural habitat is a council flat in *Skelmersdale*? Cheers.

SHAUN. It's been for ever.

DENT. I texted you hours ago, I've been waiting, I've got to go.

DENT *starts putting her shoes on.*

SHAUN. '44 Feltons'. I felt the hairs on the back of my neck stand up when I read that on the text just now, all I could hear was your high-pitched little voice when we were six. 'We've gorra learn our addresses in case we get kidnapped by a flasher!' 44 Feltons, Birch Green, Skelmersdale, Lancashire, England, Earth, The Universe. I memorised yours cos I didn't wanna be took back to mine to sit around in me pants while me ma kicks off at a pack of biscuits. I knew you'd get hold of me in the end. I would have come round before I just –

DENT. I want you to get rid of my mum's stuff.

SHAUN. What, from in here? All of that?

DENT. I'll pay you.

SHAUN. But… it hasn't been that long, you can't –

DENT. Yes it has. I don't need two people's stuff.

SHAUN. Oh. Well, nice to be of help, Little Miss Independence, suppose you don't mind asking for help when you're paying. Did you have a chauffeur in Manchester? Butler? Would Madame like a peeled grape and a panini? I know what it's like, you know, outside Skem, in poshland, people shake

hands for no reason and eat food out of the wrong stuff.
The pubs have got stupid names like The Fig and Hat Stand,
The Mansion and MacBook, The Rape and Apology.

DENT. The Rape and Apology?

SHAUN. Yeah and you eat chips off a bit of wood.

DENT. The *Rape* and Apology?

SHAUN. Aren't you pleased to see me?

DENT. I texted the number on the postcard in the newsagent.
It said 'Shaun the handyman', half of Skem is called Shaun.
I didn't know it was gonna be you.

Pause.

SHAUN. Oh.

DENT. Look, I've got to be somewhere. You crack on, I'll be
back later.

SHAUN. No.

DENT. No?

SHAUN. Your mum's stuff?

DENT. It's all broken and threadbare and fucked. Bag it up,
take it to the tip. You'll do what I pay you for.

SHAUN. What's happened to you? Dufflecoat Dave said you
had gone posh. He says you're posher than Posh Anne and
she had a dinner party. And she served meringue swans on
a bed of green jelly.

DENT. Meringue isn't posh, it's eggs. I need to go.

SHAUN. Do you need to buy a monocle?

DENT. I'm going to Ashurst Parade.

SHAUN. What for? The chippy's gone, Ethel Austin's gone,
that café's never bloody open.

Beat.

Are you going to the chemist?

DENT. No.

SHAUN. You're sick.

DENT. No.

SHAUN. You look sick. You're acting weird.

DENT. Cheers! Shaun, it's been ten years, people change.

SHAUN. What are you getting from the chemist? You're the type for Temazepam, is it that? I bet it's that.

DENT. The type?

SHAUN. A bit Adrian Mole, worrying about whether shit exists. Gripping the end of your sleeves so your feelings don't fall out.

DENT. It's not Temazepam.

SHAUN. So you *are* going the chemist! Lorazepam, Diclazepam? Is it one of the azey-pams? I can get you dog Diazepam off Dufflecoat Dave. I can get you anything really, Oxycontin, a knock-off bedpan.

DENT. Wow. I don't want anything off Dufflecoat Dave.

SHAUN. Not methadone, you're not the type for that?

DENT. How am I not the type for methadone?

SHAUN. You've got ornaments. Tramadol? Sertraline? *Prozac?*

DENT. Shaun.

SHAUN. Olanizipine?

DENT. Shaun.

SHAUN. Nortriptyline? Amitriptyline?… What.

DENT. I'm not sharing. You shouldn't take drugs unless they're prescribed to you.

DENT *puts her coat on and walks away slowly.* SHAUN *springs up and joins her.*

SHAUN. Behave.

She starts leaving.

I'll come with yer.

SHAUN *jumps up and follows* DENT *out.*

Scene Two

The chemist. SHAUN *and* DENT *sit on cramped seats inside a small haphazard chemist. They are the only ones in there. A pharmacist is out the back.*

SHAUN. What was that all about on the way here?

She glares at him.

You're walking like a geriatric flamingo.

DENT. Since when have you seen a flamingo?

SHAUN. Oh and I suppose Manchester is full of the lanky pink bastards, isn't it. I can get you a disabled bus pass. Mike the Geek knocks 'em up on his laptop.

DENT. I don't like lying.

SHAUN. Not lying though is it, you *are* disabled, you're acting it.

DENT. I went to hot yoga class last night. I used my muscles so effectively they now –

SHAUN. Don't work?

DENT. Hurt.

SHAUN. What's hot yoga?

DENT. They do it in London, it's this thing, sort of like a dinner party, except you have to make the shape of a swan with your body, and then you stretch out flat, that's called 'the

panini', and then you all eat meringue and swap
ornaments... oh and you have to wear a monocle.

Pause.

SHAUN. You're taking the piss but that'll be all the rage next
year. They'll do anything in that London if you tell them it's
in fashion. Ah, what? Not more of it, look.

He indicates a CCTV camera on the ceiling.

DENT. The CCTV camera? Big deal. They're everywhere now.
If you've got nothing to hide you wouldn't be bothered.

SHAUN. Seriously? Where have you got that from? We used to
be alright here until people started poking their noses in.

DENT. Calm down.

He stands and talks loudly to the pharmacist.

SHAUN. Ey! Love. There's no need for these cameras, you
know. You're paranoid, no one'd wanna nick any of this shit.
I know what you think of me. Watching all the time.

DENT. It's not about you.

SHAUN. You're not allowed to be broken any more.

DENT. You're talking shit.

SHAUN. Have you not watched Channel 5, *Benefits Street*,
Benefits Tenements, *People on Benefits in Bedsits in
Blackpool*, it's all they can do but put cameras on all of our
heads, like they do to dogs.

(*Talking to the pharmacist again.*) It's not *Big Brother*, we're
meant to be a fucking community.

Pause.

DENT. Okay.

Beat.

He brings the stool over and sits.

SHAUN. Not good being disabled, you know. You need to knock that off. Do you have your five-a-day? You're meant to have five-a-day.

DENT. I've heard.

SHAUN. It's gorra be proper in-the-flesh veg. You can't get 'em from the shit shop on Sandy Lane, it doesn't count if they're in a tin.

DENT. It does, actually.

SHAUN. It doesn't – (*Laughing*.) aahhh you think Fray Bentos is one of your five-a-day, no wonder you can't walk!

DENT. Piss off.

SHAUN (*still laughing*). Ah you think Pot Noodle's a fruit!

DENT. Pot Noodle's got peas in it, you prick.

SHAUN. No it hasn't.

DENT. The Beef and Tomato one has.

SHAUN. Oh yeah it does. You can get proper veg from the Paki shop.

DENT. Don't call it that! Where have you got that from?

SHAUN. Why? I don't mean it bad, that's what it is.

DENT. It's a lot of sodding things, Shaun, you don't have to choose the one word that –

SHAUN. If it was an English shop I'd call it the English shop.

DENT. Do you call Asda's the English shop?

SHAUN. No.

DENT. Well then don't call it the Paki shop then.

SHAUN. Well what should I call it?

DENT. Just call it the shop!

SHAUN. But how would you know what shop I mean?

DENT. I know what bleeding shop you mean, Shaun!

Silence, sulking.

SHAUN. I'll grow my own sodding veg then.

DENT. Where?

VOICE. Susan Matthews.

SHAUN. Fuck off!

DENT *goes to the counter.* SHAUN *sits and keeps checking the cameras and getting himself worked up, he stands up and paces like he wants to batter someone, gives the CCTV the finger, and then sits down and does slow breathing like he has been taught how to do it by someone who has never been as angry as* SHAUN *gets.* DENT *comes back distraught, showing her hands as they have nothing in them.* SHAUN *is really aggravating her now.*

What's the matter? Are they fucking you about?

DENT. I went through all this yesterday, it's pissing me off. Six months to be referred to the pain clinic and I finally get there and they're like, 'Yeah, we'll give you something stronger.' 'Can I have it then?' 'We'll write to your doctor.'

And then yesterday I was meant to come and pick it up from here and she tells me it's this recorded-drug bullshit and that I've gorra fetch the prescription from the doctor's, so I get down there, bring it back and they haven't got those tablets in, so I spend the night in bulk and we come here now and guess what, the bleeding doctor hasn't bothered to sign the sodding thing. She could have told me that yesterday. So now I've gorra go all the way back to the doctor's, get him to sign it and come back here. Ridiculous.

SHAUN. Listen, go back to yours, I'll get this signed, pick it up here and bring it to you, okay?

DENT. I'll get my tablets for myself, Shaun, thank you very much, I wasn't born yesterday.

SHAUN. I'm not gonna nick your tablets, what's wrong with you?

DENT. Nothing's wrong with me. I just don't need anyone's help.

SHAUN. Just give me the prescription.

DENT. Are you still scared of being seen with me?

SHAUN. I walked here with you, didn't I?

DENT. Yeah about half a mile ahead of me.

SHAUN. You walk slow.

DENT. And now we've gorra go through the high street, round Digmoor, down Tanhouse, past where the bandstand used to be, that's a lot of people.

SHAUN. So? I'm not bothered.

Scene Three

Outside. It is still afternoon. Nice weather. Open and pleasant. They are where the bandstand used to be. They walk a little and DENT *sits down to rest.*

DENT. What are you like, you?

SHAUN. I'm making sure that I don't get zapped by the Aspiration Dispersal Field. The generators. They're everywhere, they'll get you, you know, there's no escaping.

DENT. Machines that zap aspiration? In Skem? I can't believe people believe this shit.

SHAUN. It's real. I've googled it! The fella from The Verve did a concept album about Skem and *he mentioned it in it*. Do you think that's why you were alright? Cos you moved away were the generators weren't?

DENT. Why do you care?

SHAUN. And before that your mum protected you from it. And now she can't. That's why you're like how you are now.

DENT. If you're gonna insist on hanging round me like a fly on shit, the least you can do is shut up and enjoy the view. I just want to sit here.

Pause.

SHAUN. Tell me, at university, one thing that you learnt.

DENT. It was ages ago.

SHAUN. Shakespeare, I bet you did Shakespeare.

DENT. A bit.

SHAUN. What's he all about then?

DENT. What was the last book you read?

SHAUN (*sarcastically*). *Mr Bump*.

DENT. Well there you go. Shakespeare is like the Mr Men books, everyone has a flaw and they either get over it or they don't.

SHAUN. *One* flaw?

DENT. Yes.

SHAUN. Just one.

DENT. Shaun!

SHAUN. People are made out of flaws, otherwise there's perfect bits and that's just bollocks. Sounds like Shakespeare didn't understand people.

DENT. Well I'll be sure to pass the message on to the university English department.

SHAUN. How did you go to university? Your mam was a dinner lady in our school.

DENT. You get loans and that.

SHAUN. Like Wonga loans? I qualify for a Wonga loan, I've checked.

DENT. Look, university's shit. You know how Paul Marriot said 'integral' in school in 1996 and everyone still calls him Integral Paul.

SHAUN. So, what?

DENT. I thought university'd be full of people saying 'impinge' and 'imbecile' and 'ecstatic' and... I dunno 'postmodernism' and not being judged off it.

SHAUN. What did they call each other then if it wasn't off what they said, were they called like 'Tiara Tracy' and 'Kev the Cravat'?

DENT. They just called each other by their names.

SHAUN. Weirdos. So did no one call you 'postmodern', is that why you've got a gob on?

DENT. What do you think?

SHAUN. Did you lose your bottle?

DENT. I didn't fit in.

SHAUN. You didn't fit in here.

DENT. I didn't fit in here cos I was short. I didn't fit in there cos I'm from here.

SHAUN. What do all them words mean, 'impinge' and that.

DENT. They don't matter.

SHAUN. Why? Cos I've not been to university? I know stuff. I know loads of stuff you don't know. When I walk into a pub I can tell you how many lads there are up for a scrap, and who's the one who's got the rage and could kill you cos he doesn't give a fuck about tomorrow. I know how to make a crack pipe out of an asthma inhaler, some tinfoil and an elastic band.

DENT. That's not good stuff to know.

SHAUN. I know which shops do the cheapest milk.

DENT. Well maybe that.

Pause.

I used to love this place.

SHAUN. The bandstand?

DENT. Yeah, and Skem. Skem was daft and young and you and my mum.

SHAUN. You don't like it any more.

DENT. I started trying to get out of Skem before I could get out. I rebelled in my own quiet little way.

SHAUN. In secondary school you walked around the playground reading a book. Don't know how you got away with it.

DENT. I didn't have much choice, I was on my own then.

Pause.

Angie East and me had our first date here. I was fifteen, she was sixteen, I had a heart full of revolution and young love. We went out for two years, much to the chagrin of the school bursar. She was the first person to ever tell me 'I love you'. We sat here and held hands, felt like I was in a film, like my life had finally started, you know? Like I had found someone who actually understood me for the first time.

And then Spike Thompson's lot came on bikes and terrorised us and we had to hide in the woods, holding hands.

SHAUN. I saw my first rat here.

DENT. Shaun!

SHAUN. What? I did!

DENT. It's not very romantic, is it, a rat?

SHAUN. It's true though.

DENT. I don't care!

SHAUN. Well I thought you were having a moment and then you're going on about Angie frigging East.

DENT. Oh, here we go. You never liked her.

SHAUN. It wasn't for the reasons you think! Dent, I don't care that you fancy girls, your mam never cared that you fancy girls, girls don't care that you fancy girls, it's 2017, no one cares that you fancy girls. It's all fine now. Everything's fine!

DENT. And you'd walk down the high street holding hands with a lad, would you.

SHAUN. It's not the same.

DENT. How?

SHAUN. Because I'd be pretending.

DENT. How would you know, you've blocked yourself off to falling in love with a man because you want to fit in.

SHAUN. You've blocked yourself off to falling in love with a man because you want to not fit in. Your first kiss was with Keith Longbottom in the phone box behind the shops on Sandy Lane. You were thirteen, he was fifteen, you had a belly full of strawberry and kiwi Mad Dog 20/20.

DENT. I'm bisexual, I haven't blocked myself off to anything. I knew what I was when I was thirteen and I know now, you should trust me to know my own sexuality.

SHAUN. You should trust me to know mine then. Angie East was around for five minutes. She wasn't even funny, she smelt of Dairylea and she called you Susan. I was around for the important stuff. I spent over a year making stories with little shit puppets for you when your dad died. I distracted you from being sad for a decade. We didn't even say the word 'dad' after that. We never talked about them.

DENT. Why would we have talked about dads when we had mums? Dads are, I don't know, *they work and they die*.

SHAUN. Mine didn't.

His name's Martin Craddock and he lives in Ormskirk.

DENT. You know where your dad is?!

Pause.

When did you find this out? Have you met him? What's he like? Shaun!

Pause.

Are you worried he'd not be impressed by you? You were boss at making things, leave you alone for five minutes with a pot of Tippex and you come back to a Mona Lisa. You could paint portraits of posh women's dogs. You could do murals. Shaun, you could make figures for Wallace and Gromit!

SHAUN. My signing-on clerk in the Jobcentre, been seeing him for three years, never remembers my name, has to read it out every time, 'Purpose and meaning, Shaun, that's what you need, that's what a job will give you', will it?

Me mam used to work in Kamak, carrying boxes from one conveyor belt on to another, again and again for ten hours, go home, sleep, dream about carrying boxes from one conveyor belt to another, like overtime she's not being paid for, wake up, go to work, conveyor belt to another.

She could only carry two boxes, the lads were carrying three, sucked the life out of her, stopped laughing, it's alright if you're doing it for a year, isn't it, but for the rest of your life, anyway, she ended up on antidepressants, they sucked the colour out of her even more.

She found a pothole round the back, took a photo of it, where's there's blame there's a claim, she got as bladdered as she could on the money she had and got a hammer, held her breath, bashed her knee in with it, eight grand she got.

She said that one moment of agony bashing your knee in with a hammer is way better than a year of slogging your brain to nothing. Makes sense.

Do you remember your dad? I do. He was tall.

Pause.

You used to eat apples, you shouldn't be walking like an old woman.

DENT. I'll be better when I've had me tablets.

SHAUN. That must be why they make you do a marathon to get the bloody things. Why don't you just give me the prescription.

DENT. Because I can do it myself.

SHAUN. I'm quicker.

DENT. I'm not slow.

SHAUN. Look, everyone's shit at something, Shakespeare said.

DENT. Piss off.

Scene Four

The GP waiting room. There are lots of people around. SHAUN is sat fidgety and flustered. DENT joins him.

SHAUN. Sit down. Sit down!

Are they getting the doctor to sign it? It's half-past now. The chemist shuts at five.

DENT. Yes! What do you *think* I was asking them to do?

SHAUN. Yeah but it's rammed, half of Skem's in here, they're all after something, you've got to be assertive. Jump the queue, you're sick.

DENT. It's a doctor's, everyone's sick.

SHAUN. How're you gonna get back the chemist? You were walking like a snail then. This is stupid, I can't believe you didn't just give me the prescription. I could have done this ages ago, my legs work.

Pause.

So, what's the deal, are you gonna be sick everywhere or something. What sort of withdrawal stuff am I working with here?

DENT. Shaun.

SHAUN. Does it hurt? Do you remember Self-Deprecating Karen?

DENT. No.

SHAUN. Me neither. Does it?

DENT. Not as much as he hurts.

SHAUN. Who?

DENT. Him, look. With the brown hair.

SHAUN. Who?

DENT. There! Trackie pants on.

SHAUN. Everyone's got brown hair and trackie pants on.

DENT. In the Everton scarf.

SHAUN. What, Wheelchair Terry?

DENT. Shh!

SHAUN. What?

DENT. What do you call him that for?

SHAUN. He's in a wheelchair. His name's Terry.

DENT. Is he here on his own?

SHAUN. Why?

DENT. I think he is you know.

SHAUN. So what?

DENT. How do you know him?

SHAUN. Known him for years. He went in The Birch.

DENT. Is he like a little mascot? Does everyone buy him drinks?

SHAUN. Do they bollocks.

DENT. How does he get home when he's pissed? Does everyone help him?

SHAUN. He's a dickhead when he's pissed. Always puts The Housemartins on the jukebox. The Housemartins. Look, he

drinks Diamond, smokes Berkeley, eats pickled eggs. His
brother deals Oxycontin. He's just some fella.

DENT. Has he always been that way?

SHAUN. What, an Everton supporter? Look, he's got mates,
and people just help each other, it's nothing to do with
wheelchairs, everyone needs stuff. Wheelchair or not.

DENT. He's in a wheelchair, living his life and going the
doctor's on his own. I'm still upright and I'm scared to leave
the house. I'm a frigging hermit.

Pause.

SHAUN. A hermit? I didn't know you were a hermit. Is that
why you've never had a proper – (*Whispers.*) Cos you're
a hermit? Sorry. Makes sense.

DENT. Well, it's more complicated than that, isn't it, it's not
that I don't like people I'm just not great at – hang on, what
do you think a hermit is?

SHAUN. You know – (*Whispers.*) you've got a minge, and then
next to it you've got yer tackle and your little testes hanging
down?

DENT. Fucking hell.

SHAUN. It's alright, I won't tell anyone, I like you being weird,
I'm weird.

DENT. You're thinking of a hermaphrodite, a hermit's someone
who doesn't leave the house much.

SHAUN. Oh! Sorry, sorry, I didn't mean to mention your minge,
I'm not interested in it, I mean, not in a bad way. I just like…
you're more interesting than a minge.

DENT. Thanks!

SHAUN. That came out wrong, I just mean, some people are
too beautiful to penetrate, you know what I mean?

DENT. Wow!

SHAUN. I didn't mean that, I just, look, I don't want to fuck
   you, okay.

DENT. Shh.

   Pause.

SHAUN. I don't know what you've had to pretend to be in
   Manchester but you can be all fucked up in Skem. You can
   be a hermit, you can be disabled, have a laugh, just don't be
   snooty. I'm all fucked up and no one's bothered. I was in the
   Scarisbrick ward for four months once, but you can't be
   precious over it.

   I had this mate, Graham, we found Jenga and got the giggles,
   imagine Jenga in there where everyone's got the shakes.
   Every time I said 'Jenga' to him after that he'd laugh his
   cock off.

   When I first went in right, it was that summer when Jedward
   first came out, and I had my eyes shut for days, everyone
   thought I was blind but it's just the sedation, isn't it. They
   had to give me *shitloads* of it. Soon as I open my eyes,
   frigging Jedward everywhere, on telly, in magazines, going
   on with themselves with their fucking hair, and I was off me
   head, I didn't know what was real, and I thought Jedward
   was a symptom of my psychosis.

   Pause.

   But they don't make tablets to make Jedward go away,
   do they.

DENT. Are you okay now?

SHAUN. I was okay then! I wasn't in because I was mental, it
   was a misunderstanding. I just get angry.

DENT. You get angry? What like?

SHAUN. Do you know about when Grayson Perry came and
   did that telly programme here, it was about masculinity,
   couldn't bear to watch it just in case, makes my blood boil,
   people don't understand that one person's trying doesn't look

the same as theirs. So all these cameras. I know what they're thinking, you know.

I love Skem and it pisses me off when people look at it wrong. They've got their own filters on their eyeballs. We know what we're doing,

It's no wonder I kick off.

VOICE. Susan Matthews?

DENT *gets up, slowly.*

Susan Matthews?

DENT. Coming!

SHAUN. It's twenty-to.

DENT *collects the prescription.*

You're never gonna make it. Give it to me.

DENT. I have spent my life doing everything for myself.

SHAUN. Big deal, so have I. So has everyone, you're not special.

SHAUN *exits.*

Scene Five

SHAUN *returns with a commode.*

SHAUN. Dent!

DENT. Where'd you get that from?

SHAUN. Round the back. Get in.

DENT. No fucking way.

SHAUN. Why not?

DENT. It's a commode.

SHAUN. It's got wheels.

DENT. So's a wheelbarrow and you don't expect me to go around in one of them.

SHAUN. You can't afford not to. Eighteen minutes-to.

DENT. I didn't ask you to get that for me. I'm not getting in it.

SHAUN. This'll get us to the chemist in ten minutes, then back to yours, we'll have a cup of tea in time for *Tipping Point.*

DENT. I can make my own decisions, I'll ask you if I need help.

SHAUN. That won't work cos you won't ask.

DENT. Well I'm asking you now to fuck off with the walking.

Beat. She walks a little.

SHAUN. Just lean on it. Like a Zimmer frame.

DENT. I'm not an old woman.

SHAUN. Sorry, sorry. Like a shopping trolley then.

Beat.

See, that's better, isn't it?

She walks, slowly.

You need to speed up though.

DENT. Sod off.

SHAUN. Sixteen minutes.

SHAUN *and* DENT *face centre-stage.*

They walk.

SHAUN *hums the beginning of the* Super Gran *theme tune.*

SHAUN *whistles the next part of the* Super Gran *theme.*

SHAUN *sings the next part of the* Super Gran *theme.*

SHAUN *and* DENT *sing the last line together.*

You think you're a lone wolf. You've just had a hard time that's all, it makes people –

DENT. What?

SHAUN. Crabby. Hard to be around.

DENT. Funny(!). Doesn't explain the minute we went to high school you wouldn't be seen dead with me.

SHAUN. I walked home with you every day.

DENT. Only cos none of your proper mates lived round here.

SHAUN. 'Proper' mates? I hated them.

DENT. Hated them? You had a ball with Steve Lyons and Matt Jones and all that lot of no-marks, what are they doing now? I hope they're rotting away in bedsits, lonely and self-loathing and riddled.

SHAUN. I never bullied you.

You know that time when we were thirteen, and Ginette Middleton rang you at home and your mum said you were in bed, but that you might not be asleep yet, you might be reading in bed?

And then Ginette told everyone and they laughed their heads off at you and after that your nickname was –

BOTH. Susie Dent.

SHAUN. Well it was me that gave you that nickname, to stop them calling you something crueller.

DENT. Like when you called me a 'freak, lesbian, vile, dwarf cunt'. You showed your true colours then.

SHAUN. I don't know what to say.

DENT. I believe 'sorry' is traditional.

SHAUN. Look, fifteen-year-old lads, they're all dickheads, it's part of the job description. You have to fit in. You can't get by if you don't fit in.

DENT. Do you bollocks!

SHAUN. Gary Caffrey got a job in Peacocks, he had to wear a shirt and tie, and he'd hide it in a bag and get changed in work to save himself the hassle of getting battered. John Cragglefish had a schoolbag that was slightly bigger than normal and they made his life hell. This is how it works for lads: you do anything a bit weird, you get battered. You show any weakness, you get battered. You show you care about anything, you get battered.

DENT. And being a woman is a toddle, isn't it? Especially me.

SHAUN. You're allowed to be clever, you're allowed to be weird, you can be anything you want.

DENT. Women earn fifteen per cent less than men.

SHAUN. Stop being statistics at me!

DENT. I just happen to know more than you!

SHAUN. No you fucking don't! I can't believe you say that. You're a selfish arrogant cow!

DENT. Selfish? My mam bought you Christmas presents, we took you to Blackpool every year.

SHAUN. On your birthday.

DENT. I had to lie to my mam about you ignoring me in school. I pretended it was all fine for five years cos I didn't want to let her know her golden boy was a cunt.

SHAUN. You can't be mates with a girl in high school, especially one like...

DENT. Me?

Pause.

You can't be friends with scabby little lads in primary school but I was! No one else would hang round with you so I got stuck with you. You had scabies in school, Shaun, you had fleas. Every day, you pestered me to let you have the tinfoil off my butties from my packed lunch and I'd give you it every day, and you said you wanted to make sculptures from the tinfoil for your mum to make her love you.

When I was little I never realised how weird that was, it was my mum who explained it to me. 'Tinfoil,' she said to me with her eyes wide. 'Why did we have to give Shaun his dinner half the time? Why did I buy him school shoes and take him to Blackpool with us?' And then she told me.

Your mum was a junkie. She loved smack more than she loved you.

SHAUN. Fuck off.

SHAUN *freaks out.*

Do you know how it felt, your mam helping me? Someone who gave a shit. Made your tea and cared. Do you know what I thought was gonna happen? I thought she was gonna have me living at yours. I thought she gave a shit about me, and what happens next? 'Sorry, Shaun, but my daughter's future is too important, it's her exams and we need to think about her exams.' How stupid was I? You can get your own prescription on your own. Fuck off!

He leaves. DENT *is getting very tired and slow. She starts to lose her balance. She staggers. She falls.*

DENT. Shaun!

SHAUN *returns.* DENT *holds out the prescription.*

Pause.

SHAUN *takes it.*

Scene Six

The flat. It gets increasingly dark outside.

We hear Last of the Summer Wine.

SHAUN. Wankers. Closing five minutes before closing. I mean, how stressed can they be? 'Oh here you go, Tina McKinnley, here's a big bag of hormones, hope you enjoy them; sorry, Stinky Bob, didn't see you there, here's something to put lead in your pencil, what do you want, Dr Kilner, you want me to do something for you, well fuck off.'

DENT *doesn't respond.*

I can get dog Diazepam off Dufflecoat Dave.

It calms you down. Makes you not care.

DENT *doesn't respond.*

I can ring Wheelchair Terry's brother

Hearing-Aid Kev

Get you some Oxycontin

DENT *doesn't respond.*

Do you want a pillow?

I can fetch the duvet off the bed.

Are you allowed Lemsip?

Are you allowed a hot Vimto?

Are you allowed toast?

Are you allowed hot stuff or cold stuff or both? Or neither.

Are you allowed a cappuccino? I can't make them anyway.

Are you allowed to speak?

Do you want me to read you a story?

Dent!

Look, I can't help you if I don't know what's wrong with you, can I.

Are you just gonna ignore me?

Pause.

SHAUN *finds the postcards.*

'Dear Mum, me and Miles are having a splendid time.' Miles? 'Splendid'?

Beat.

DENT. Never mind, you.

SHAUN. What's his second name? Prower? Miles Prower. 'We went to a mass in the Basilica San Marco.' What's that when it's at home?

DENT. It's a cathedral.

SHAUN. You used to giggle through mass in school.

DENT. That's cos you'd do silly voices.

SHAUN *does a silly voice.*

SHAUN. 'Lord, I am not worthy for you to enter my gaff, but just say the word and I shall be healed.'

That's funny.

DENT. Will you give them to me, they're private.

SHAUN. Hang on.

DENT. Actually I would like a cushion, and some water.

SHAUN. Right, Dent, you peculiar little chap of a girl, my personal Adrian Mole, I'm gonna get you through this. We need to make an inventory of stuff you've got that will ease the pain.

DENT. I'm fine.

SHAUN. Listen! This is my superpower, if you put me on *Mastermind* this would be my subject.

SHAUN *finds items and being them into the living room.*

Right, your extra-special Shaun-made pile of 'Get Me Through the Night'… shite. We have one bottle of cider. One quarter bottle of Advocaat, there's no lemonade to go with it, but there is… Irn-Bru!

Continues to find stuff.

Plus, ibuprofen, aspirin, St John's wort, Crème de Menthe, an ornament of a bunny being friends with another bunny, and Bully's top prize: one video of *Button Moon*.

And not to be a cliché but I can see that there's a tenner behind the clock.

DENT. The tenner for the leccy?

SHAUN. Ten pounds. Boss, we're rolling in it, princess.

Twelve cans of Kestrel

Chips and spam fritter for two

Fifty bags of Space Raiders

An E and a Sherbet Dib Dab

DENT. No. Ten glowsticks. They're only a pound.

SHAUN. We could get a mix of all the good stuff in that shop. Marshmallows.

DENT. Felt tips

SHAUN. A lightly dented tin of stewed steak

DENT. Lemon sherberts?

SHAUN. Strawberry laces

DENT. A Ginsters pie

SHAUN. Dandelion and burdock

DENT. Graph paper

SHAUN. Beef and Tomato Pot Noodle!

DENT. Frazzles!

SHAUN. Two-pee shrimps!

DENT. Brillo pads

SHAUN. Nine-pee noodles

DENT. Ginger nuts

SHAUN. Peperami

DENT. Wagon Wheels

SHAUN. Popping candy

DENT. Mushroom Cup a Soup

> *Suddenly. The lights go out. The leccy has gone – the electric meter has run out of money.*

> Shit! The leccy's gone.

SHAUN. Should I put the emergency on?

DENT. That was the emergency.

SHAUN. You knew it was going to go?

DENT. I forget things.

SHAUN. So much for living like kings.

> *Pause.*

> You know Scabby Annie?

DENT. Yes

SHAUN. Well I heard her once boasting on the bus that when the leccy goes she'll always spend her last fiver on cider instead of putting it on the meter because you can either sit in the light or drink in the dark.

> *Pause.*

> But.

> *Pause.*

> I'm scared of the dark.

DENT. Me too.

SHAUN. I'll go the shop, get a tin of leccy!

> SHAUN *leaves.*

Pause, she sings the first couple of lines from the theme tune of Button Moon. *She trails off.*

Pause.

She takes a big breath and starts singing again at a higher volume and energy as at the start of the singing she just did, this time she keeps the same energy and doesn't descend into sadness.

She starts redoing the dialogue (and voices) from the earlier episode of Last of the Summer Wine.

SHAUN *comes back, wearing some fairy lights. He walks up to where* DENT *is sat.*

Bad news, no leccy, after five, isn't it, everyone's been by now.

DENT. Shit!

SHAUN. It's okay though, look! (*Switches on the fairy lights.*) Plus I've got you shitloads of bits, and a scratchcard!

DENT. What did you get that for? It's just throwing money away.

SHAUN. No it's not. Anyway, the money from scratchcards is donated to like, art.

DENT. There's no art round here.

SHAUN. There's all that sculptury shit on the roundabouts.

DENT. A black cuboid and a load of old rocks?

SHAUN. There's that mental metal daffodil. Look, normal people, they buy a scratchcard and they just scratch it there and then. What have they bought for themselves there? A moment.

DENT. Of disappointment.

SHAUN. A moment of disappointment. But us, we're not normal, are we?

DENT. No.

SHAUN. We'll only scratch one now and then, when you need it. Some people scratch it away and then lose. And we're gonna wait a whole evening.

DENT. And then lose.

SHAUN. Yes.

DENT. Why?

SHAUN. Cos them silly buggers down the shop, they buy themselves a second of hope. What are we doing? We're buying ourselves a whole night of hope.

DENT. That's quite good actually. It's like tantric sex. But with carbon-coated cardboard.

She scratches one square.

Fifty thousand pounds.

SHAUN. It's good for the mind.

Okay leave it now.

He grabs it off her. SHAUN *starts to unpack his bag from the shop.*

DENT. You've taken loads of shit off me today, you've been patient, you've tried to do the right thing in your own fucked-up way.

SHAUN. Yeah, I've been pretty boss, haven't I, took loads of shit, I've *provided*… I was trying dead hard. I think I've been a saint.

DENT. You nicked a commode.

SHAUN. Exactly.

DENT *starts to get down from the sofa.*

Here, I'll get it for you.

DENT. No, just put the stool by the drinks for me.

She sits on the stool.

SHAUN. What would madame care to eat? We have Space
     Raiders, Kit Kats, choccy biscuits.

DENT. I'll have the Space Raiders.

SHAUN. And what would madame like to drink? Would she
     like to try the Shaun special?

DENT. What's the Shaun special?

SHAUN. Secret recipe.

DENT. In that case I think I'll just have the Irn-Bru. Quiet here
     tonight. Have a drink on me.

SHAUN. Thanks very much.

He pours himself a drink.

BOTH. Cheers!

SHAUN. To your mam.

Pause.

DENT. I gave up my job, came back here. I'd been saving up to
     go to Iceland to see the Northern Lights for Miles's thirtieth
     birthday. But Mum couldn't look after herself. When I turned
     up she was sat in a wheelchair but had no one to push it. He
     dumped me while I was here. He said Skem was to blame for
     me not fulfilling my potential so I told him to do one.

SHAUN. Wanker.

DENT. He was actually. He grew cress and thought it mattered.
     Thank fuck for that holiday money cos it meant I could stay
     here. She didn't look like my mum. All the colour had
     drained out of her. I lay on the couch watching *Last of the
     Summer Wine* with her for days. I'd never realised what that
     phrase meant till then. She kept losing bits, then laughing.
     The last thing that she said to me was, 'You can start living
     your life again, buggerlugs. Why don't you get a haircut, put
     a colour on it, get some new clothes off the market, get
     yourself some make-up and get your arse out to The Birch.
     It's about time you meet some nice young thing, make sure

they've got nice eyes, a good heart and a lovely arse.' And then she just died. The last word she said was 'arse'.

Beat.

SHAUN *bursts out laughing.*

Fuck off!

SHAUN *tries to speak but he can't stop laughing.*

Piss off.

DENT *smiles. She starts laughing too. They laugh for a bit.*

Pause.

How quick can you get Oxycontin?

SHAUN. Just got to text him. I can get you dog Diazepam –

DENT. I'm not taking anything prescribed for dogs!

Is Oxy addictive?

SHAUN. If they keep fucking up your tablets it will be.

DENT. Is it expensive?

SHAUN. Pound a tablet. I know you got these morals about lying and not taking stuff that isn't prescribed to you but we're nice, not criminals, sort of.

SHAUN *takes out his phone and waggles it in front of* DENT. *She nods.*

Look, Steve Lyons, remember him? He'd do anyone's benefits form for a pint of Diamond down at The Birch. He'll help you get on your disability benefits. Then things will be easier, you'll have money, you can get taxis and bread and milk and cut-price custard creams –

DENT. I've tried already to get disability benefits. The PIP form is like a dissertation on how shite you are. Then being interviewed on how shite you are, asking questions on toilet problems, in this tiny room, being poked as if you're guilty when all you are is fucking suffering. They even wrote my height down wrong.

SHAUN. We'll do it again.

DENT. I can't face it. People like me are at the bottom of the
pile. And it's getting worse. Once they scrap the NHS you'll
be in the same boat as me.

Beat.

SHAUN. There's this dead-good thing this fella told me in the
woods once, you know the weird woods in Birch Green near
the van that doesn't move? He said that you go through life
right and you come to a river so you make a raft to like, get
on, and then you carry that raft around for the rest of your
life even though you're just walking on the ground then like,
no river, and you could put it down, but you don't.

Beat.

But there's loads of rivers round here, isn't there. That's why
you have to learn to swim.

DENT. Shaun, why did you come?

SHAUN. I'm a handyman.

DENT. Shaun...!

Beat.

SHAUN. I'm going to have a son.

DENT. What? How?

SHAUN. How?

DENT. Who helped you?

SHAUN. Who helped me?

DENT. Oh my god.

SHAUN. What do you think?

DENT. Oh my god!

SHAUN. Do you think I'm gonna be a shit dad?

DENT. No. Who's the mum?

Beat.

SHAUN. Lisa Henderson. From school. It's complicated, but I'm trying to prove myself innit. I'm learning to swim. I'm gonna do this online book-keeping course, off Groupon. I've been looking at the information on food packets, seeing what's good for you. I'm being a good person.

DENT. When's he due?

SHAUN. She's seven months gone now. I'm not gonna be one of them dads that just do the fun stuff though, I'm gonna do the discipline and stuff as well. And I'm gonna make sure he knows who I am.

Not like my dad. I did meet him. He turned up late and bladdered. He was just some fella. Some dickhead. But you know how you build up things in your head.

DENT. Maybe he was really nervous.

SHAUN. No. He just wasn't interested.

DENT. I'm sorry.

SHAUN. It's okay. I walked away, I just thought 'What a loser', and I wasn't angry. Dent, I can't have my son feel like that about me.

Pause.

DENT. Okay. You're gonna be a dad!

SHAUN. Shit.

DENT. Fuck. You're gonna have to have rules.

SHAUN. And teach him stuff.

DENT. Teach him to shave.

SHAUN. I'm gonna have to say 'flip' instead of 'fuck'.

DENT. It's the end of days!

SHAUN. And I'm gonna teach him about the rivers and the rafts, make sure he's not too rafty, but just rafty enough.

DENT. I can teach him words. We can teach him about Skem.

SHAUN. Yeah, cos we know what it's about.

DENT. And people who don't think it's a shithole.

SHAUN. And you.

DENT. Think it's my inheritance.

SHAUN. Yeah, might teach him about Pokémon instead of all that first.

DENT. Good idea, what else?

SHAUN. Don't eat white poo?

DENT. Don't drink your neighbour's snow?

SHAUN. The shop on Sandy Lane has the cheapest milk.

DENT. Expect people to be homophobic, in a nice way.

SHAUN. Memorise your address in case you get kidnapped by a flasher.

DENT. Don't throw something away just because it's broken.

SHAUN. Don't be mean to fumbling people.

DENT. People can fly when you don't make them feel self-conscious about it.

SHAUN. You can only piss with the cock that you've got.

DENT. Pot Noodle's got peas in it.

SHAUN. Don't cut your face in spite of someone else's face.

DENT. Don't cut off your face.

SHAUN. Watch your fuckin words.

DENT. Five-a-day.

SHAUN. Freeze bread.

DENT. Get your leccy before five.

SHAUN. You can cope in the dark if you're with your bell-end mate.

DENT. See, we know stuff.

SHAUN. Too right we know stuff, we know loads of stuff. We've got loads of rafts. We're excellent weirdos. We're cosmic scallies.

DENT. We dance on the off-beat.

SHAUN. We're wonky shopping trolleys.

DENT. We're forgotten and trod on.

SHAUN. We're gravy-stained and piss-sodden.

DENT. We're the breath between coughing fits.

SHAUN. We're subnormal.

DENT. All wrong.

BOTH. Beautiful wankers!

The End.

A Nick Hern Book

Cosmic Scallies first published in Great Britain in 2017 as a paperback original by Nick Hern Books Limited, The Glasshouse, 49a Goldhawk Road, London W12 8QP, in association with Graeae and the Royal Exchange Theatre, Manchester

Cosmic Scallies copyright © 2017 Jackie Hagan

Jackie Hagan has asserted her moral right to be identified as the author of this work

Cover photograph by Gu Photography; title artwork by Dragonfly Design

Designed and typeset by Nick Hern Books, London
Printed in Great Britain by Mimeo Ltd, Huntingdon, Cambridgeshire PE29 6XX

A CIP catalogue record for this book is available from the British Library

ISBN   978 1 84842 711 2